Cape Buffalo and Oxpeckers

by Kari Schuetz

BELLWETHER MEDIA • MINNEAPOLIS, MN

Note to Librarians, Teachers, and Parents:

Blastoff! Readers are carefully developed by literacy experts and combine standards-based content with developmentally appropriate text.

Level 1 provides the most support through repetition of high-frequency words, light text, predictable sentence patterns, and strong visual support.

Level 2 offers early readers a bit more challenge through varied simple sentences, increased text load, and less repetition of high-frequency words.

Level 3 advances early-fluent readers toward fluency through increased text and concept load, less reliance on visuals, longer sentences, and more literary language.

Level 4 builds reading stamina by providing more text per page, increased use of punctuation, greater variation in sentence patterns, and increasingly challenging vocabulary.

Level 5 encourages children to move from "learning to read" to "reading to learn" by providing even more text, varied writing styles, and less familiar topics.

Whichever book is right for your reader, Blastoff! Readers are the perfect books to build confidence and encourage a love of reading that will last a lifetime!

This edition first published in 2019 by Bellwether Media, Inc.

No part of this publication may be reproduced in whole or in part without written permission of the publisher. For information regarding permission, write to Bellwether Media, Inc., Attention: Permissions Department, 6012 Blue Circle Drive, Minnetonka, MN 55343.

Library of Congress Cataloging-in-Publication Data

Names: Schuetz, Kari, author.
Title: Cape Buffalo and Oxpeckers / by Kari Schuetz.
Description: Minneapolis, MN : Bellwether Media, Inc., [2019] | Series: Blastoff! Readers. Animal Tag Teams | Audience: Ages 5-8. | Audience: K to grade 3. | Includes bibliographical references and index.
Identifiers: LCCN 2018033939 (print) | LCCN 2018034672 (ebook) | ISBN 9781681036830 (ebook) | ISBN 9781626179530 (hardcover : alk. paper)
Subjects: LCSH: Mutualism (Biology)–Juvenile fiction. | African buffalo–Behavior–Juvenile fiction. | Oxpeckers–Behavior–Juvenile fiction.
Classification: LCC QH548.3 (ebook) | LCC QH548.3 .S35 2019 (print) | DDC 577.8/52–dc23
LC record available at https://lccn.loc.gov/2018033939

Table of Contents

Eating Together

Three oxpeckers hold on to a Cape buffalo as it **grazes**. The birds pluck **ticks** from the buffalo's back.

Suddenly, the birds start hissing. They have spotted danger!

Cape buffalo and oxpeckers call the **plains** of Africa home.

Tag Team Range

☐ = Cape buffalo and oxpecker range

There, they use **symbiosis** to make survival easier. Together, the animals give and receive help.

hoof →

Cape buffalo are big **mammals** that walk on **hooves**.

type: mammal

height: up to 4.9 feet (1.5 meters)

length: up to 11 feet (3.4 meters)

weight: up 1,910 pounds (866 kilograms)

life span: 20 or more years

Thick, hook-shaped horns crown their huge heads. These sharp growths become weapons when the buffalo fight.

The buffalo roam plains in search of food and water. These **herbivores** feed on grasses and drink from **watering holes**.

Cape buffalo herd at a watering hole

They travel in **herds** to stay safe from lions and other **predators**.

Oxpeckers are small birds with red or yellow beaks. Sharp claws on their toes give the birds a strong grip.

Red-billed Oxpecker Profile

type: bird
length: 8 inches (20 centimeters)
weight: 1.75 ounces (50 grams)
life span: up to 15 years

Long, stiff tail feathers help them keep their balance.

Oxpeckers are **insectivores** that perch on large animals to eat.

They peck at pests in the animals' fur. Several birds may feed on the same animal at once!

Helping Each Other

Cape buffalo bodies draw many **parasites**. Luckily, oxpeckers love to eat these ticks and other pests.

They help the buffalo stay healthy. In return, the birds get tasty meals!

Cape buffalo also give
oxpeckers rides on their backs.
The birds prefer riding to flying.

In return, the birds look out for predators. They warn the buffalo about nearby danger.

Tag Team Trades

Cape buffalo

provide meals

give rides

oxpeckers

eat pests

watch for danger

Cape buffalo and oxpeckers
have an unusual friendship.
They work together to survive.

The buffalo keep the birds well fed.
The birds help keep the buffalo
from danger!

Glossary

grazes—feeds on grasses

herbivores—animals that only eat plants

herds—groups of Cape buffalo that travel together

hooves—hard foot coverings

insectivores—animals that eat insects

mammals—warm-blooded animals that have hair and feed their young milk

parasites—living things that use other living things to survive; parasites harm their hosts.

plains—areas of flat land with few trees

predators—animals that hunt other animals for food

symbiosis—a close relationship between very different living things

ticks—bugs that attach to skin and suck blood

watering holes—pools of water from which some animals drink

To Learn More

AT THE LIBRARY

Jenkins, Steve, and Robin Page. *How to Clean a Hippopotamus: A Look at Unusual Animal Partnerships.* Boston, Mass.: Houghton Mifflin Books for Children, 2010.

Reyes, Gabrielle. *Odd Animal Helpers.* New York, N.Y.: Scholastic, 2011.

Rustad, Martha E. H. *Zebras and Oxpeckers Work Together.* Mankato, Minn.: Capstone Press, 2011.

ON THE WEB

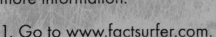

Factsurfer.com gives you a safe, fun way to find more information.

1. Go to www.factsurfer.com.

2. Enter "Cape buffalo and oxpeckers" into the search box.

3. Click the "Surf" button and select your book cover to see a list of related web sites.

Index

The images in this book are reproduced through the courtesy of: Four Oaks, front cover (Cape buffalo); Michael Potter11, front cover (oxpecker left), p. 12; Nico Fourie, front cover (oxpecker middle); Susan Liebenberg, front cover (oxpecker right); Janugio, p. 4; Jean-Jacques Alcalay/ Biosphoto/ Alamy, p. 5; Angelo Cavalli/ Getty Images, pp. 6-7; Peter Betts, p. 8; Benny Marty, p. 9; Arco/ TUNS/ Alamy, p. 10; NSP-RF/ Alamy, p. 11; Erni, p. 13; Jason Gallier/ Alamy, p. 14; Gail Shotlander/ Getty Images, p. 15; imageBROKER/ SuperStock, p. 16; Gallo Images/ Alamy, p. 17; michaeljung, p. 18; Hannes Thirion, p. 19 (left); EdenF, p. 19 (right); 2630ben, p. 20; Safari_Pics/ Alamy, p. 21.